Colonial New England

by Barbara Wood

Editorial Offices: Glenview, Illinois • Parsippany, New Jersey • New York, New York
Sales Offices: Needham, Massachusetts • Duluth, Georgia • Glenview, Illinois
Coppell, Texas • Ontario, California • Mesa, Arizona

Every effort has been made to secure permission and provide appropriate credit for photographic material. The publisher deeply regrets any omission and pledges to correct errors called to its attention in subsequent editions.

Unless otherwise acknowledged, all photographs are the property of Scott Foresman, a division of Pearson Education.

Photo locators denoted as follows: Top (T), Center (C), Bottom (B), Left (L), Right (R), Background (Bkgd)

Opener: DK Images; 1 Dorothy Littell Greco/The Image Works, Inc.; 3 DK Images; 4 Alamy Images; 5 Dorothy Littell Greco/The Image Works, Inc.; 6 DK Images; 7 David Lyons/DK Images; 8 Cary Wolinsky/Stock Boston/Aurora Photos; 10 DK Images; 12 DK Images

ISBN: 0-328-13349-3

Copyright © Pearson Education, Inc.

All Rights Reserved. Printed in the United States of America. This publication is protected by Copyright, and permission should be obtained from the publisher prior to any prohibited reproduction, storage in a retrieval system, or transmission in any form by any means, electronic, mechanical, photocopying, recording, or likewise. For information regarding permission(s), write to: Permissions Department, Scott Foresman, 1900 East Lake Avenue, Glenview, Illinois 60025.

3 4 5 6 7 8 9 10 V0G1 14 13 12 11 10 09 08 07 06

In the year 1607 the first English colonists came to Jamestown, Virginia. Let's travel north from Virginia and farther ahead in time.

It is 1650. We are in colonial New England. Most of the settlers have come from England by ship. To them, this place is a "new" England.

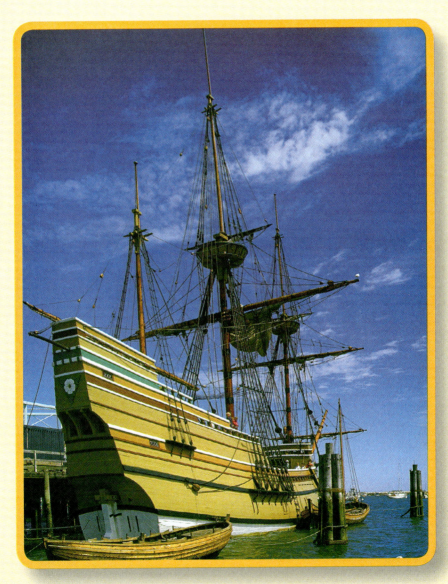

New England colonists have to make almost everything themselves. When they need clothes, they make yarn from sheep's wool. Next they weave the yarn into wool cloth. Then they sew the cloth into clothing.

Colonial women sewing and visiting

Men and boys in colonial New England wear short pants, called breeches. They wear long stockings that go to their knees.

Girls and women wear long wool skirts and aprons. Outdoors and indoors, they wear caps called coifs.

Clothes in colonial New England

Most of the homes in colonial New England are like the cottages that the colonists lived in back in England. They are made of wood boards. They have steep, thatched roofs.

An English cottage

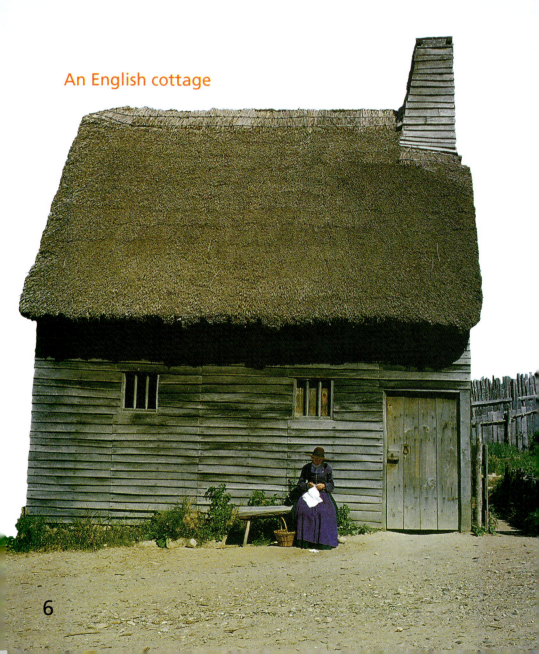

The cottage has only one room. It is called a keeping room. The family cooks, eats, works, and sleeps in the keeping room. There is a fireplace for warmth and for cooking.

In most families everyone sits on rough benches or small barrels. They hang their clothes from pegs on the wall. The children's beds are bags filled with straw.

A keeping room

The colonists grow corn and other vegetables. Much of the corn is ground into cornmeal for making cornbread.

Colonial families drink milk from their goats. They eat bacon and ham from their pigs. They get their eggs from the chickens they raise.

Preparing a meal in colonial New England

There is no refrigerator in 1650. Meat must be salted or smoked so that it does not spoil. Apples are sliced and hung to dry. Vegetables are stored in a cool, dirt cellar under the ground.

There is always much to be done here in colonial New England. Farm animals need food. Fields need clearing before corn can be planted. Candles must be made.

Older children help clean the home, weed the gardens, and carry wood. They are in charge of scaring the crows away in the cornfields.

A busy colonial village

Colonial boys and girls learn to read and write. Boys learn job skills by working with craftsmen. Girls are taught other skills at home such as sewing and cooking.

Children in the New England colonies might have fewer toys than you do. But they play games and have fun, just as you do!

Let's return to the present and think about our visit to the past. If you had been a colonial child, you would have worked hard. You would have learned some different skills than you are learning today.

Do you think you would have liked living in colonial times? It's interesting to think about living at a different time in our country's history.

Traveling back in time at Plimoth Plantation